NO GOOD MEN
Things Men Do That Make Women Crazy

by Genevieve Richardson

Illustrated by Rick Detorie

A Wallaby Book
Published by Simon & Schuster, Inc.
New York

Acknowledgments

Special thanks to Marilyn Wabby, Melissa Newman, JoAnn Butler Braff, Candis Coffee, Linda Goldin, Debra Leventhal, Karen Scarborough, and Laurie Stockdale for their dedicated assistance in the research of this enormous project.

Genevieve Richardson is a full-time philosopher and a part-time waitress. Her previous writing credits include the soon-to-be-published *Nothingness and a Side of Fries* and the Off-Off-Off Broadway musical *Hey, Spinoza*. She lives in Venice, California.

They hog the covers.

They say they'll call, but never do.

They leave their dirty laundry knotted and inside-out.

They criticize you when you disagree with them.

27

33

After the third date they become cheap.
ARE YOU REALLY GOING TO EAT ALL THAT?

They let things grow on their shower curtains.

44

They leave their fingernail and toenail clippings all over the place.

49

They splash.

They forget the "little things."

60

They put empty containers back into the refrigerator.

They brag about their sexual performance.
ARE YOU KIDDING!? I'M GREAT IN THE SACK! SHE CAN'T GET ENOUGH OF ME.

They never throw out their old clothes.

They_____
_____

(FILL IN THE BLANKS)